"She shall be called
WOMAN"

ANNEKE KAAI
MARY MIKHAEL

PiQUANT
editions

First edition, first printing
This edition copyright © 2009 by Piquant Editions Ltd
PO Box 83, Carlisle, CA3 9GR, United Kingdom
Website: www.piquanteditions.com

ISBN–13: 978 1 903689 60 8

British Library Cataloguing in Publication Data
Kaai, Anneke, 1951-
"She shall be called woman".
1. Kaai, Anneke, 1951-
2. Women in the Bible–Art.
3. Women in the Bible–Biography.
I. Title II. Mikhael, Mary.
759.9'492-dc22

Cover image(s) by Anneke Kaai: *Lydia* and *Miriam II*
Photographs of Anneke Kaai by Adri Boogaard-Both
Design by Blueprint IT Works Inc.
Printed in Italy

Contents

* portrait with abstraction

Photo by Adri Boogaard-Both

Anneke Kaai

Anneke Kaai was born in Naarden in the Netherlands in 1951. Her gift for painting and drawing was clear from a very young age. After school she trained first at the Gooise Academie for Fine Arts and then at the Gerrit Rietveld Academie in Amsterdam.

Anneke has painted several series of works based on biblical themes through which she has developed her expressive personal 'abstract and symbolical' style. Previous series include 'Creation', 'Apocalypse', 'The Ten Commandments', 'The Psalms', 'Relating to God' and 'Bible Words'. There is a list of her published works at the end of this book. The portraits here are more representational than the works in her other recent series and, in that, represent a slight departure from her established style.

Anneke's art is unashamedly Christian and biblical in its inspiration and content. Her paintings are regularly exhibited in churches across the Netherlands and she has been invited to present her work at international Christian conferences abroad. It is her desire that viewers will experience something of the power and spiritual reality of God, who inspires her, when they come face to face with her paintings.

I dedicate the paintings in this book to three women who are close to my heart:

my daughter Riegonda,

my daughter-in-law Gieneke,

and my granddaughter Ruthy—Anna Ruth Sofia.

I also want to express my deep thanks to everyone who has supported me in so many different ways during the process of bringing this beautiful book to birth.

Anneke Kaai, 2009

Mary Mikhael

Mary Mikhael is the first ever woman president of the Near East School of Theology in Beirut in Lebanon. She is also the Associate Professor of Education at NEST and an elder in the Presbyterian Church of Beirut. She directed the women's programme of the Middle East Council of Churches (MECC) and has been involved in the leadership of international women's associations such as the Fellowship of the Least Coin and the World Day of Prayer. She is a widely travelled international speaker and a writer.

Mary is particularly dedicated to training, inspiring and supporting women in Christian ministry as well as in wider social leadership. She holds an Ed.D. from Columbia University and the Union Theological Seminary in New York City, USA. Her biblical understanding is informed by the rich and ancient spiritual traditions of the church in Lebanon.

The meditations that accompany the portraits in the English edition of this book are drawn from a series of reflections on biblical women that Mary wrote in 2008 for this particular project.

Introduction

The thirty paintings of key biblical women in this collection depart from the typical abstract and symbolical style for which the artist, Anneke Kaai, has become known through most of her previous series of biblical paintings. During the 1990s she painted three individual portraits of biblical women, but only more recently was she able to expand them into a full series of portraits. Through study and meditation on the associated biblical texts, she sought to 'know' each woman thoroughly before setting out to present her in a direct way that communicates with viewers today. Some of the portraits clearly show the influence of Anneke's early classical academic education. She has painted these faces in a realistic manner, using contemporary materials and forms. Other portraits are depicted in a more abstract-expressionistic manner. Some women are depicted as shaped by one controlling emotion—of love, hatred, joy, fear, anger, hope. Others are literally 'cut in two', seamlessly combining opposite, competing emotions into one likeness.

The series as a whole reveals a great variety of interpretations and painterly techniques. It has been a personal quest for Anneke that has tested her expressive vocabulary. Four of the paintings form diptychs with accompanying 'abstractions' that distil the pure emotions depicted. They relate closely to Anneke's more established style of working. Although those portraits and abstractions form a unity in each case, they can also be exhibited as separate works.

The paintings are all 60x80cm, in acrylics, sometimes with mixed media, on plexiglas. Their sequence in this book is arranged for visual impact rather than according to biblical chronology. It is the artist's hope that viewers will be motivated and moved, and that they will find much that resonates with their own experience as they come face to face with these biblical women.

In the accompanying texts, Mary Mikhael extracts poignant moments from each woman's life. In a manner similar to that of the artist, she also meditated on the biblical texts in order to get to 'know' each woman. Her insights instruct and inspire as they reflect both common realities of life in the Middle East today and general observations about women's lives, aspirations and frustrations everywhere. Readers will glimpse how these women reacted to the struggles, fears, challenges and joys they faced. In particular, readers will come to a deeper understanding of how someone's faith in God, or the absence of it, shapes their actions, for good or evil, and may have results that ripple on long after their earthly life has ended.

Eve

Adam named his wife Eve, because she would become the mother of all the living.

Genesis 3:20

Eve is my mother. Eve is my sister. I am Eve.

Despite the fact that every human being descends from Eve (in the painting her iris combines hues of brown and blue), our first response to her is often negative. In the Middle East, for example, a man shouts Hawaa ('Eve') at a woman if he wants to express contempt, that he sees her as deceitful, weak or easily led astray. The church fathers expressed similar views. When I think of Eve, I prefer to imagine the moment Adam opened his eyes: 'Wow! Bone of my bones and flesh of my flesh—woman!'

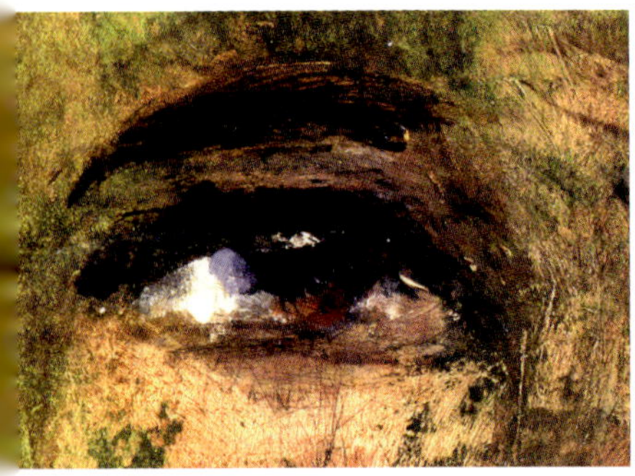

When Eve disobeyed God's instructions in Eden, Adam was with her. And God's response was clear: instead of rejecting Eve, God sanctioned enduring enmity between her and the serpent. And Adam named Eve not for her role in bringing death into the world but in hope, looking forward to her role as the promised bearer of new life and, ultimately, of the One who would finally crush the serpent. Adam was given no parallel title, for God alone is the Father of the living.

The painting shows two sides to Eve's face—on the left, peace and joy as she lived with Adam in Eden; on the right, sadness and anxiety as they faced survival outside the garden. Motherhood is a blessing that brings burdens. Yet children are God's gift. They embody hope, new life, a new beginning, a future.

God, our Father, who loves all humankind with the love of a father and a mother, we praise your name! Giver of life, help us to value and nurture life.

Miriam I

His sister stood at a distance to see what would happen to him.

Exodus 2:4

A young girl stands near the riverbank. She is looking intently at a basket floating among the reeds. Inside it is her three-month-old baby brother. It is not clear how old she is—maybe around eight years of age? Old enough to understand what is at stake, but wise enough to stay at a safe distance. This is no game. It is a desperate deed, an extreme experiment in hope. This is life or death. And the girl is very afraid.

Is she considering what will happen to the baby if he survives? Or is she worried that the basket might draw water and sink, and that her little brother will drown before she can reach him? Probably both. Can she imagine that Pharaoh's daughter will come and save him and adopt him as her son? Not a chance! Is the river calm, or is there a strong breeze blowing over the water? Are the reeds swaying, rubbing and squeaking against the precious basket? And how long has she been waiting there? Did her mother instruct her to keep watch or was this her own idea? Where is her mother? We simply don't know. But we can all put ourselves in the shoes of that frightened young girl, her heart bursting with love, concern, fear, anxiety, and wild hope for a sheer miracle to intervene . . .

Thank you, Lord God, for the hope that strengthens our faith: that you are the one who saves, whatever our circumstances. Help us to be bold, even when we are afraid, because of that hope. Strengthen our faith.

K'05

AK '98

The Wife of Pilate

While Pilate was sitting on the judge's seat, his wife sent him this message: 'Don't have anything to do with that innocent man, for I have suffered a great deal today in a dream because of him.'

Matthew 27:19

What 'dream' moved this woman to interrupt Pilate during an important judgment? Was she given a glimpse that the events of that day, rather than an unfortunate misruling, kindly forgotten by history, would become a refrain repeated down the centuries: 'Jesus Christ, God's only son, our Lord … suffered under Pontius Pilate, was crucified and died …?' A chilling nightmare indeed.

Some say that we relive experiences of the day in our dreams. Perhaps Pilate's wife had met Jesus? Did she know about his acts of mercy, healing the sick and raising the dead, touching the untouchables and restoring them to full humanity? Did she know about him feeding the hungry, opening the eyes of the blind, teaching with authority and doing miracles that subdued nature and cast out evil spirits? Or had she only heard about him and longed to meet him? Surely, then, she suffered even more over the next three days, after Pilate had washed his hands in mock innocence even as he was granting the crowd their demand to 'Crucify him, crucify him!'? I like to imagine her among the women who went to Jesus' tomb on Easter Sunday morning, and then saying to Pilate over breakfast: 'You too, you can repent, for He is risen—He is risen indeed!'

God, thank you for your reality. Thank you that when you see a heart that is open to you, you come in and fill it with hope that casts out sadness.

Rebekah

So they called Rebekah and asked her, 'Will you go with this man?' 'I will go,' she said.

Genesis 24:58

This portrait shows two sides to Rebekah. On the left is a young girl, both excited about and daunted by the life-changing decision she faces. On the right is a vague impression of her as a bride, for her future is unknown . . .

'I will go.' How could a young girl make a decision like that with such apparent ease? Was she so keen to get married? Was she tired of living in her father's house, doing the work of a servant? Did she long for adventure? Or was it wealth that attracted her? Eleazar had generously given her 'a ring in her nose and bracelets on her arms'. Was it not dangerous to go off with someone she had just met in order to be married to a person she had never even seen? Or could it be that she had fallen in love with Isaac just by hearing about him? No doubt Abraham's servant, Eleazar, spoke eloquently about his masters, and about the wealth Isaac would inherit. Did he also tell Rebekah about Isaac's miraculous conception and birth? Or did Rebekah know the God of Abraham and sense his call? In that case, her decision expressed a bold step of faith—involving real risk yet undergirded by absolute trust that all would end well.

O God, help us trust your plans for our lives. We do not know our future, but you know everything and hold the past, the present, and the future in your hand as Lord of history and time. Help us surrender to your will and show us when to step out in faith.

The Medium at En-Dor

When the woman saw Samuel, she cried out at the top of her voice and said to Saul, 'Why have you deceived me? You are Saul!'

1 Samuel 28:12

This is a woman who lives in the shadows. Eleven times the biblical writer calls her simply 'the woman'. God hates her profession, and earlier King Saul had banned its practice. But, at the lowest point in his life, King Saul burns to know the future. Waiting can often be so painful. So the king disguises himself and finds a guide.

The woman is suspicious of her midnight visitor's illegal request. Does he not know it can lead to death! Or is he setting a trap for her? Only when he swears by the Name of the Lord does she consent. It is easy to imagine the chilling terror with which she realized that she had been cheated, by the very one who is bound by law to take her life! Do I blame her or sympathize with her? God knows, I feel sympathy for her, yet I think she got what she deserved. Was she bribed? Was it her habit to accept bribes? Or was she enslaved by her practices?

It is not easy to condemn this woman. When she sees the king's desolate state she is more concerned about his welfare than her own. She insists on serving him without a hint of gloating. Was she good or evil? Like all of us, she could be both. Only the power of God and God's love can make good overcome evil in us, as we keep in step with the promptings of God's Spirit.

O God Almighty, cleanse us by your Holy Spirit.

Ruth

'Where you go I will go, and where you stay I will stay. Your people will be my people and your God my God. Where you die I will die, and there I will be buried.'

Ruth 1:16–17

It would feel to me as if I were stepping into a deep, dark hole if I had to leave all I know and love in exchange for an unknown place and people. The left side of Ruth's face in this portrait shows her deep agony at leaving her country, culture and people. The young Moabite widow had decided to cling to the old Hebrew widow. Both women had lost all that they loved most in this life. Ruth's words echo as a model for any loving, lifelong commitment. The right side of the portrait reflects Ruth's inner strength, faith, faithfulness and hope. There could be no return to Moab for her.

What better stories can a mother tell her family than the stories of the mighty acts of God, who rescues the oppressed and marginalized, hears the cries of the needy and feeds the hungry? The stories of a faithful, loving God, a God one can trust. Compared to him, whatever you treasured most in the past is clearly seen to be worthless. Were those the stories Ruth heard Naomi tell? And, had Ruth known that she would one day be among the ancestors of the Messiah, would she have recorded a Magnificat too—in honour of God, not Boaz, who had covered her with his mercy?

God of Naomi and Ruth, you are great and you move in mysterious ways to save and to rescue. You deserve our devotion and praise—no one who follows you ever regrets it. Help us to trust you with our lives.

Jezebel I

[King Ahab] also married Jezebel daughter of Ethbaal king of the Sidonians, and began to serve Baal and worship him . . . Jezebel was killing the prophets of the Lord.

1 Kings 16:31; 18:13

Jezebel is portrayed here as a beautiful and strong but proud and stiff-necked woman. She was born as a princess in the Sidonian court and was a staunch Baal worshipper. She was anti-God and anti-Israel. It did not take her long to get King Ahab to worship Baal. It seems hard to believe that any woman could be so cruel and manipulative. In her wily seduction of Israel's king, Jezebel embodies an enmity against God that reminds us of the ancient serpent that tempted Eve.

Jezebel was not superstitious or easily frightened. She did not baulk at callously killing the prophets of the Lord in an attempt to obliterate the worship of the living God from Israel. Even Elijah's spectacular demonstration of the power of God when pitted against the impotence of the prophets of Baal did not frighten her in the least. On the contrary, her vicious threats and commitment to revenge terrified Elijah into fleeing and hiding away and plunged him into depression. In the face of her malice, he felt isolated and God-forsaken.

We are more used to powerful men ruling with such self-absorbed cruelty. Jezebel reminds us that evil is not bound by gender; every person who wields power must denounce the temptation of corruption and greed.

Lord God, we pray that you will make us sensitive in the use of power, in whatever context you grant us leadership or influence. Help us to do right and to live humbly as your servants.

The Wife of Potiphar

She caught him by his cloak and said, 'Come to bed with me!'

Genesis 39:12

The deceitful wickedness of this woman is in stark contrast to the faithful integrity of her servant Joseph.

He is a stranger in the land; she is the wife of an influential, wealthy man. She can have whatever she wants; he is a slave. He is satisfied; she is not. He does not desire what he cannot have; she wants whatever her eyes desire and she is shameless in pursuing her greed. Deep tones of yellow and red in the portrait express passionate desire and envy. One can imagine Joseph's shock when she first approached him. Relentlessly, day after day, she persisted. For Joseph there was no 'grey' area: to sin against his master, who trusted him completely, would be to sin against God. But the wickedness of this woman did not allow for her plans to be thwarted. If she could not have him, she would ruin him. Lust and arrogance blinded her and she became like a brute beast. Remorselessly she destroyed his reputation, and, without any recourse to justice, he was thrown into prison.

We know that God had much greater plans for Joseph, plans which made his prison stay necessary. He eventually became one of the most powerful men in Egypt. No one knows what happened to Potiphar's wife—she disappeared off the stage of history without a name or further mention, remembered only as a foolish, lustful, unfaithful and wicked woman.

God Almighty, help us not to fall into the temptations of lust, greed or lying words. Help us to be faithful—first to you, and second to serve others faithfully too, with compassion and love.

Miriam II

Then his sister asked Pharaoh's daughter, 'Shall I go and get one of the Hebrew women to nurse the baby for you?'

Exodus 2:7

Moments earlier, this young girl had been hiding at a distance, very frightened. Where did she suddenly get the courage to approach a royal princess and address her with such a daring suggestion?

It is often noted, even today, that a sister's love and concern for the safety and welfare of the boys in her family come close after a mother's devotion. This girl was keeping watch on the riverbank for a purpose: she was a partner in God's plan of salvation for her people. Was that day a turning point in her life, an unforgettable personal experience of God's direct, awesome saving power?

Later in Genesis we get to know her as Miriam and find out that she was part of a leadership trio, with Moses and Aaron, for the newly rescued Israelite people. Particularly after the Israelites' miraculous escape across the Red Sea, Miriam emerged as a prophetess and she led the women singers and musicians in praising God. She understood salvation. Did she remember then how it had started on the riverbank, that day, when an Egyptian princess fell in love with a Hebrew slave's baby boy? When a young girl—a clever, wise, loving, brave sister with one passion only—was there for the purpose of getting her baby brother home to his mother?

Thank you, God, for placing us in families. Help us to be 'sister' or 'brother' to everyone who needs our care and courage. Thank you, God, for moving in mysterious ways to save and protect your people.

Delilah

Then [Delilah] said to [Samson], 'How can you say, "I love you," when you won't confide in me?' . . . When Delilah saw that he had told her everything, she sent word to the rulers of the Philistines . . . to subdue him.

Judges 16:15, 18, 19

'Delila' in Arabic means a female guide (e.g., a tourist guide). The word is also used to describe a woman who cheats—particularly one who is unfaithful to her husband.

God chose Samson before he was conceived to be a Nazarite who would deliver Israel from her Philistine enemies. How could he become so infatuated with the beautiful Delilah, a wicked and calculating Philistine woman? Did Samson naively presume that his Nazarite status would guarantee God's protection despite the fact that he betrayed his Nazarite vow?

Delilah appears as the prototype seductress. Her faithfulness to her own people is unwavering. She unashamedly tricks Samson again and again to help the Philistines overpower him. The portrait shows her two 'faces'—on the left is the coquettish look that captivated Samson. The right reveals her scheming and showing her true feelings for him. The abstraction expresses stabs of intense emotion against a dark background. Did Delilah understand that in battling Samson she was really pitting herself against God, attempting to thwart his plans?

Each of us is capable of leading a destructive, two-faced life. We might even rationalize our behaviour. We do it whenever we pretend to be someone we are not.

We confess, Lord God, that we often pretend to be someone we are not. Forgive us. Help us to be people of integrity and honesty, to be faithful and committed to love and care for those who need us.

Naomi

'Don't call me Naomi,' she told them. 'Call me Mara . . . I went away full, but the Lord has brought me back empty.'

Ruth 1:20–21

'Naomi' means 'pleasant'. In submission to her husband, she left her home and people to become a refugee in Moab (lit., 'spiritual desert'). When her husband and grown-up sons died, she was left bereaved, a widow in a foreign land, a person without identity, hopeless and helpless. When she hears that God had restored bread to his people, she decides to leave her spiritual desert and walk back to Bethlehem (lit., 'house of bread').

What woman has not felt similar desperate and conflicting emotions of faith and despair at some time in her life? Despite Naomi's loneliness, fear and hopelessness, she is compassionate towards her daughters-in-law. She is gentle and honest, not wanting to inflict further suffering on them: 'I can give you no hope, but God can give you hope and have mercy on you.' The portrait shows her deep sadness at having to part from them.

Arriving in Bethlehem does not take away her bitterness. Naomi is wrapped in her own pain and bereavement. She appears harshly unthankful towards Ruth, who becomes their breadwinner, marries and bears a son who in turn becomes the great-grandfather to King David and an ancestor of Christ. The flecks of gold in the abstraction hint at that great future and at God's saving presence.

Thank you, God, that your love brings hope to the hopeless. You never disappoint those who trust in you. Your gift of grace is beyond our comprehension. Draw us close to yourself, that we may leave our spiritual desert and become part of your house of bread!

AK'06

Mary

'Do not be afraid . . . You will conceive and give birth to a son' . . . 'I am the Lord's servant,' Mary answered.

Luke 1:30, 31, 38

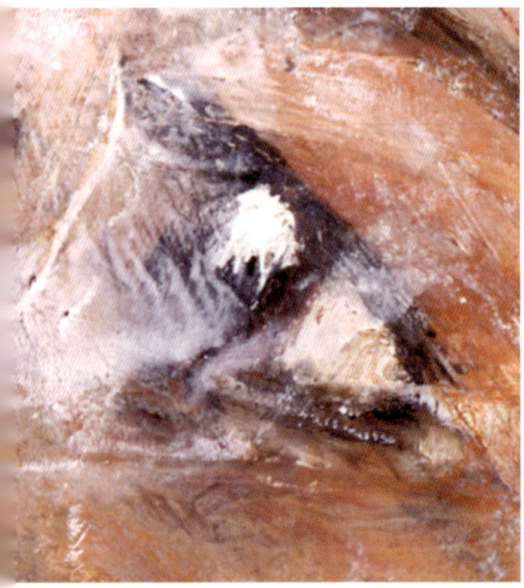

We would understand if Mary had been bewildered by Gabriel's words, if she thought she did not hear correctly or that he had picked the wrong person. But Mary understood the message. It had nothing to do with hearing rightly but everything to do with faith. Someone once remarked that it seemed as if Mary already carried the Messiah inside her well before Gabriel talked to her.

Had I been in her place, I might have asked why, if this was from God, he did not stick to the natural way of conception? But Mary understood instinctively that there could be nothing 'natural' about the Incarnation. God does what God wills—she only needed to know what was required of her.

It is impossible not to compare her response to that of Zechariah—the old, married priest who had been praying for a son for so many years. When the same Gabriel tells him that his prayer has been answered, Zechariah first wants to check the facts: 'How can I be sure of this?'

We call Mary 'blessed'. But we are the blessed ones because God used her; her obedience became the counterpart to Eve's disobedience. Where Eve failed, Mary succeeded; Eve caused our pain, but Mary participated in God's plan for our healing. At long last the traitorous serpent's head will be crushed.

Our souls magnify you, Lord! We see your saving power and we are inspired by Mary's bold trust and obedience. Help us to magnify you with our lives, whatever it costs.

AK'05

Sarah

So Sarah laughed to herself as she thought, 'After I am worn out and my lord is old, will I now have this pleasure?'

Genesis 18:12

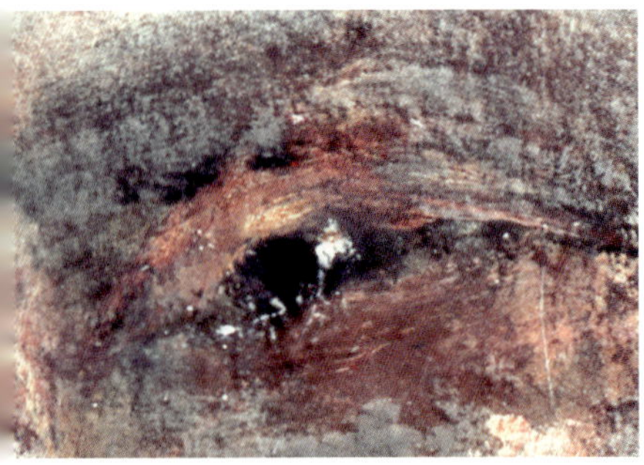

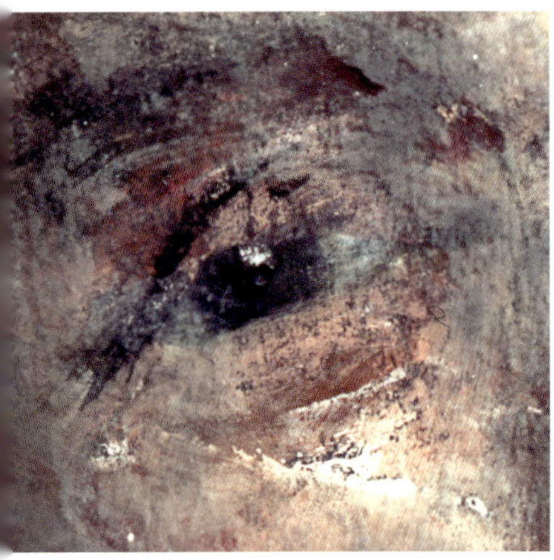

At ninety years of age, Sarah hears that she is going to conceive and give birth to a son despite having been barren all her married life. She laughs. Of course! A chuckle of inner pleasure at the preposterous idea? A nervous laugh of fear? A confident laugh because God had vindicated her at last? She would give her husband an heir. She laughs with righteous joy.

Sarah did not have an easy life. She lived as a nomad and stranger in a foreign land. Her husband, though wealthy and important, was at times a weak man. And with her barrenness so obvious, she suffered much. Did she know God's promise that, through her, Abraham would have an heir who would become the father of a vast people? Was that why she accepted her trials and honoured her husband faithfully?

The apostle Peter calls her an example of godliness and Paul refers to her as the mother of the children of promise. I confess that I wish Sarah had treated Hagar and Ishmael (whom she named) more humanely. That her treatment of them proved to be part of God's plan is hard for me to understand. But it also humbles me because, despite her apparent weakness, God blessed Sarah and, through her, even I am blessed today.

God of miracles, you choose those who are weak and fallen. You fill them with faith to see things that have not yet taken shape and use them as instruments to achieve your purposes. Thank you for your forgiveness and wisdom. Thank you that your promises always come true.

Esther

So [King Xerxes] set a royal crown on her head and made her queen instead of Vashti. . . . But Esther had kept secret her family background and nationality.

Esther 2:17, 20

This story reminds me of the story of King Shahrayar and Shahrazad in The Arabian Nights—it reads like a fairy tale. Yet it has a long tradition as part of the Jewish Scriptures as well as the Christian canon.

My first reaction is to admire Vashti, who was prepared to lose her position as queen rather than be humiliated by the king. Esther, on the other hand, appears willing to do whatever it took to please the king.

Having arrived in the palace, Esther learnt fast. As a direct result, the king chose her to become his new queen. The portrait shows her as a young woman on the brink of life, shyly glowing with excitement. At the same time she is filled with apprehension, aware of her tenuous position and secret identity.

When the crisis came and her darkest fears were realized, she requested a fast. Did she understand fasting as prayer? Was she relying on God to rescue her? When the fast paid off, she and Mordecai planned an excessively harsh revenge on their enemies. I prefer to remember Esther as the beautiful and courageous young woman who consciously risked her own life in order to save her people.

God, forgive us when we gain power and forget mercy. Help us learn from the gentleness of Jesus, the Lamb who was slain to give us everlasting life. Bless every person who gives up their own life in order to save someone else. Give us your wisdom and compassion when we face difficult decisions.

Anna

Coming up to them at that very moment, she gave thanks to God and spoke about the child to all who were looking forward to the redemption of Jerusalem.

Luke 2:38

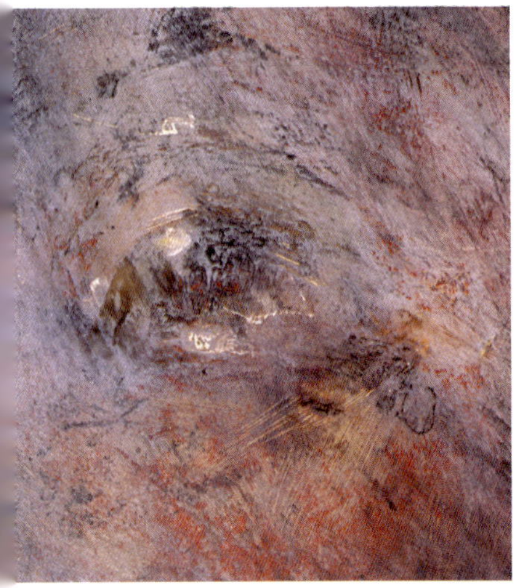

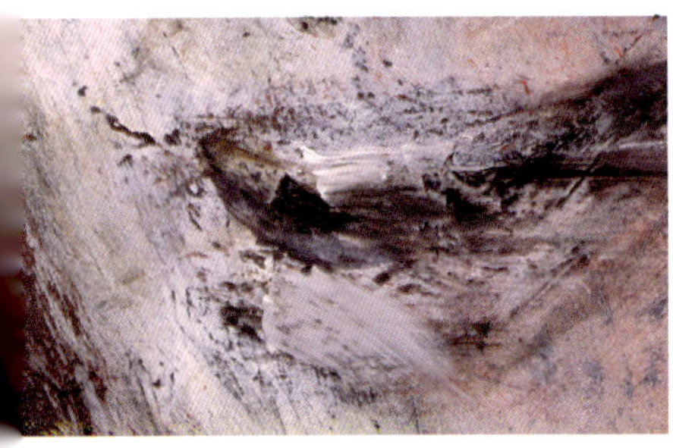

Anna is the first woman prophet recorded in the New Testament. As a widow, she lived in the temple—worshipping there day and night, with fasting and prayer. Her marriage may have been planned for her; she chose her life in the temple.

Did she live there by herself, or was she part of a community of devout believers? She must have known the psalm of the Korahites, 'How lovely is your dwelling place, Lord Almighty! My soul yearns, even faints, for the courts of the Lord; my heart and my flesh cry out for the living God' (Psalm 84:1–2). She must have sung it often, encouraged by the promise of God's protection: 'Whoever dwells in the shelter of the Most High will rest in the shadow of the Almighty. They say of the Lord, "He is my refuge and my fortress, my God, in whom I trust"' (Psalm 91:1–2).

When Mary and Joseph brought the infant Jesus to the temple that day, Anna heard Simeon's song of praise. He had seen the Lord's Messiah. How could she keep quiet? No one who meets Jesus can remain silent and keep the good news to themselves. The years of waiting, the years of preparation, had borne fruit. Anna was overjoyed—she recognized the Lord she had been waiting for.

Lord, in the midst of your gathered, expectant, waiting people is the place of your blessing and love. Help us to experience beauty in worship, prayer and fasting. Come soon! We long for you, our living Lord Jesus.

Vashti

But when the attendants delivered the king's command, Queen Vashti refused to come. Then the king became furious and burned with anger.

Esther 1:12

The book of Esther raises difficult issues. Many women are treated as little more than objects in the schemes and politics of men. Besides, the Medes and Persians were all absolute subjects of the king. In that context, Vashti's disobedience was a bold challenge. The portrait shows her as a determined woman, tinged with sadness because she must have realized that dire consequences were likely to follow her decision.

Some interpret the text to mean that Vashti was asked to strip naked in front of the king and his guests, who were most likely intoxicated. If that was the case, we must respect her bold refusal. Others interpret the king as being fair in his request that she honour him by joining his celebration instead of presiding over her own event. He was proud of her and wanted his guests to admire her. Did Vashti refuse to be treated like a precious object, risking dismissal rather than losing her self-respect? She must have been aware, too, of her influence as a role model for others—a point that the king's advisors pressed. Esther certainly learnt from her example.

I have deep compassion with Vashti. I respect her courage. Was she humbled or comforted subsequently to know that her refusal and dismissal had been instrumental in a salvation much bigger than the saving of her own dignity as a woman?

God, help us when we face dilemmas. Give us courage to act with dignity. Help us to discern what it means to lose our lives in order to gain life.

Mary Magdalene II

'Woman, why are you crying?'...Thinking he was the gardener, she said, 'Sir, if you have carried him away, tell me where you have put him, and I will get him.'

John 20:15

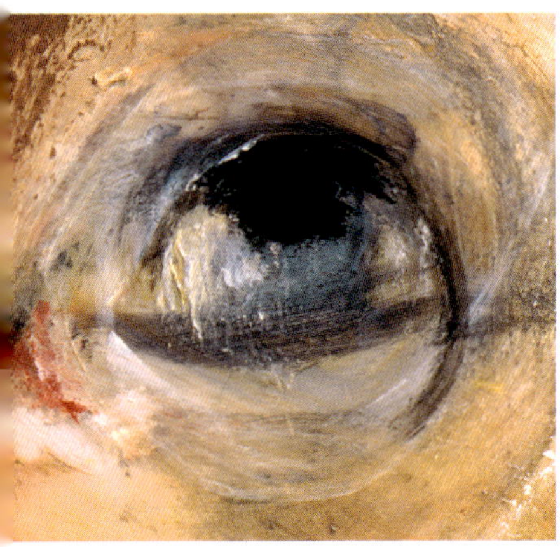

Mary Magdalene loved Jesus. He had drawn her out of deep darkness and restored her to full humanity. The abstraction expresses how her devotion to Jesus shaped her life.

No doubt she had not slept since Jesus' arrest. Earlier she had gone to the tomb while it was still dark and, on finding the stone removed, ran to Simon Peter and the other disciple (probably John): 'They have taken the Lord out of the tomb, and we don't know where they have put him!' Now she is back at the tomb by herself. The portrait shows two sides to her face—one is drawn with grief and blinded by tears, the other looks up at the 'gardener' with a shimmer of hope despite her overwhelming sadness.

'Miriam!'—'Rabboni!' Her eyes cleared, her heart leapt. What a glorious moment! All she could think of was to hug him, to hold him as tightly as possible. Mary was blessed. One of the first to know about the Resurrection, she was an eyewitness of the risen Lord. Her life had been transformed—from dark to light, from sorrow unto death to inexpressible joy—as she glimpsed everlasting life. Yes, she was blessed and greatly honoured.

O, risen Lord, I worship you. As Mary heard you call her by name, let me hear you saying my name. Fill me with joy that I may tell the good news of the Resurrection. Lift me out of my darkness into your light.

Leah

'Now at last my husband will become attached to me, because I have borne him three sons.'

Genesis 29:34

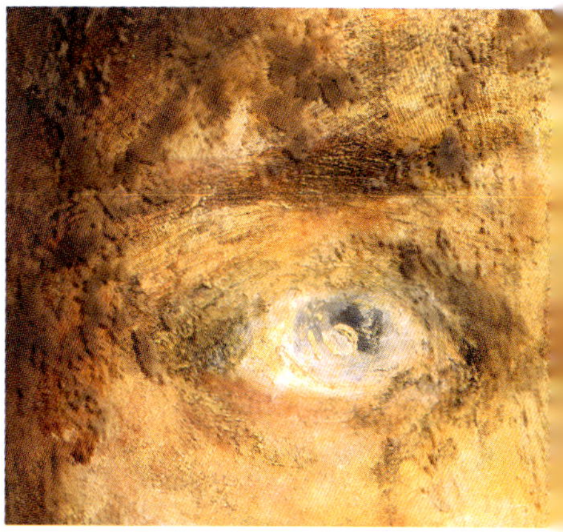

Love shaped Leah's life as much as it did Rachel's. But in Leah's case it was shaped by the absence of reciprocal love. Her suffering moves us with deep compassion. Was she a victim of her culture or of her manipulating father's schemes? Or did she collude to marry the man who was passionately in love with her sister? We are not told.

We can only guess what the morning was like after Jacob discovered he had been married to Leah. Did Leah feel victorious, proud, happy? Or was she filled with self-hatred, ashamed at Jacob's disappointment and her deception? Seven days later, her sister, the beloved one whom Jacob had longed for throughout those seven years, joins the marriage.

Leah suffered much—there was no sparkle in her eyes. The abstraction expresses her desperate grasping after elusive love. But God saw her plight and gave her sons, while Rachel remained barren. Leah never gave up hope that her husband would soften towards her because of the children she bore him; Rachel was filled with fear that her husband would stop loving her because of her infertility. Unhappiness multiplied through their rivalry, amplified down the generations. Yet God chose that broken and dysfunctional family to become the people through whom God would reveal his mighty plan of salvation.

Lord God, when our culture pressures us to behave in ways that turn our values upside down, give us godly wisdom to make the right decisions. Guide our choices and strengthen our wills, especially when we have to do things that go against the grain of our culture.

K '06

Deborah

[King] Barak said to her, 'If you go with me, I will go; but if you don't go with me, I won't go.'... ten thousand men went up under his command. Deborah also went up with him.

Judges 4:8, 10

We do not read of many woman leaders in the Old Testament. Deborah stands out in that patriarchal society as a judge and prophet—both positions that few men achieved. She was a leader of great faith, a mother to her people with authority and inner strength who was capable of inspiring hardened soldiers. And she was a singer and poetess.

Empowered by the Spirit of God, she did the work of reconciliation traditionally reserved for male elders of the community. On God's command she instructed Barak, the general of Israel, to gather an army and meet the Canaanites in battle. A strange discussion followed in which Barak demanded that Deborah go with him into battle. Was he afraid? Was it a test? Did he doubt his own authority and ability to inspire the soldiers with confidence? Did he rely on her charisma and wisdom? Deborah mocked his lack of faith. The honour of victory would not go to Barak. Instead, God would bring his enemy down through the hands of a woman!

How often God surprises us with his choices—it makes no difference to him whether he chooses a man or a woman. He looks for faith. Deborah understood that she was an instrument in the hand of God. Victory and glory belonged to God alone.

Lord, our God, how strange your choices can seem to us. How easy it is for us to question your wisdom. Forgive us. Help us trust you completely. We want to honour you. Have mercy on us.

Bride of Christ

'Come, I will show you the bride, the wife of the Lamb'. . . a radiant church, without stain or wrinkle or any other blemish, but holy and blameless.

Revelation 21:9; Ephesians 5:27

Revelation 19 uses the image of a wedding celebration as the best approximation to express God being finally united with his redeemed people from every tribe and nation and language. This 'bride' combines the skin tones of all the races of humankind.

In that 'marriage' there will be no arguments, no hard work to please the spouse, no doubts about whether the relationship is working. The bride of the Lamb, who is the Son, enters into a joyful, eternal reality of praise. She has been purified and sanctified and dressed with garments of holiness. She has been made ready to share in the victory of the Son by the glorious resurrection of those who have believed the Word, lived in hope and love, spread the gospel, fought the good fight, finished the race and kept the faith. The bride is crowned with a tiara of righteousness. She is bound in love and faithfulness to her Lord and filled with everlasting praise: hallelujah to the Father, Son and Holy Spirit, one God for ever and ever!

O bride of Christ, your struggle in the world is not in vain. Look forward to the time when there will be no more suffering—just everlasting 'hallelujah' as you are united with your Saviour and Lord.

O God, no suffering and no joy in this world can ever measure up to the joy we shall know when we finally meet you in our resurrected flesh. Help us to live with that hallelujah already in our lives—even here, today.

The Daughter of Jairus

'Stop wailing,' Jesus said. 'She is not dead but asleep.'

Luke 8:52 cf. Mark 5:41

A desperate father and ruler of the synagogue, whose only daughter is dying, turns to Jesus for urgent help. It appears that Jesus is distracted by the crowd, oblivious, and wasting precious minutes. Then, the dreaded message: Jairus's daughter, dead. Too late! Deeply saddened and confused, Jairus has nothing more to lose as he takes his chance and trusts Jesus' words: 'Do not fear'. But he must have shuddered when they finally arrived home to find a crowd of wailing mourners, people who would know a dead body when they saw one. Jairus had believed Jesus could heal his daughter. But did he believe that Jesus could raise her from the dead?

In the portrait the young girl, dumbfounded, is caught between the horror of tasting death and the joyous surprise of being restored to life and to her family. Reborn. Awake. Alive. At twelve years of age, poised on the threshold of womanhood, her life is filled with promise. Like the outcast woman suffering from bleeding whom Jesus had allowed to interrupt him on his way, the girl was given a new life! Jesus' sense of timing, though it appeared unfocused, was perfect for meeting the needs of both the privileged who came to him for help as well as those on the margins of society and apparently at the end of their 'useful' life.

O Jesus, your power restores our humanity and rescues us from death. You snatch us from the jaw of Satan who seeks to destroy us. Help us get up and live to bear witness to you, the living Lord of life.

Orpah

Then Orpah kissed her mother-in-law goodbye . . . 'back to her people and her gods.'

Ruth 1:14, 15

Orpah is overshadowed in this story by Naomi and Ruth, two strong women who had come to extreme decisions. Orpah did what she felt was right to do. She decided not to become a refugee but rather to return to her mother's home. Why take unnecessary risks? It was hard enough to be a widow without making it worse by undertaking a dangerous journey to a strange land with no promise of a better future there. Naomi had wisely held out no false promises. Orpah decided to face the devil she knew rather than the one she didn't. Don't we all think like that at times? Let us not be too harsh on Orpah.

Orpah made a legitimate choice. She turned back. The portrait shows her facing the opposite direction, full of sorrow, blinded by her sadness and, perhaps, by her limited vision. It was a costly choice, for she too had loved Naomi. I wonder whether she was just not courageous enough to face such a big change? Was her situation in her home country more fortunate than Ruth's? Had she heard the same stories about God that Ruth had heard? Did she prefer safer gods, ones she could see and touch? It is easy to judge. But what would I have done had I stood in her shoes?

How often, Lord, we are confused by the choices we face. Please guide us at such times that we may choose wisely. Help us to be courageous when we need to take risks, to accept the consequences and bear our responsibilities with faithfulness, and to be open to correction.

Rahab

'Yes, the men came to me, but I did not know where they had come from . . . Go after them quickly. You may catch up with them.'

Joshua 2:4–5

The story of Rahab is significant one. Rahab was a prostitute who lived on the fringes, by the wall of the city, marginalized by her society. She was a seasoned liar. And she betrayed her city. So why is she mentioned in Scripture alongside a hero of faith such as Joshua?

The Jewish Talmud treats her with great respect. Is her story included to show that Israel was not supposed to be an exclusive community but rather an inclusive one? A community defined by one common denominator, namely faith in God? For while Rahab cannot claim morality or integrity, no one can deny that she had faith in God. She had put her hope in him. She understood that her city was doomed and that she needed to be saved. So she cleverly bargained with the spies and sealed a covenant with them that safeguarded her life and the lives of her family. The sign of that covenant would be a crimson cord hanging from her window—a chilling reminder of the 'thread' of blood of the Passover lamb that diverted death away from the Israelite homes in Egypt. By faith, Rahab was saved, and her faith extended to her family. God had pulled her out of her desperate situation and given her a firm foundation.

Faith is a gift from God. And by faith we accept that gift and respond with love to the Giver. We praise you, God, in whom we find our hope and salvation, and by whom we are placed in the community of the faithful.

Lydia

'If you consider me a believer in the Lord,' she said, 'come and stay at my house.'

Acts 16:15

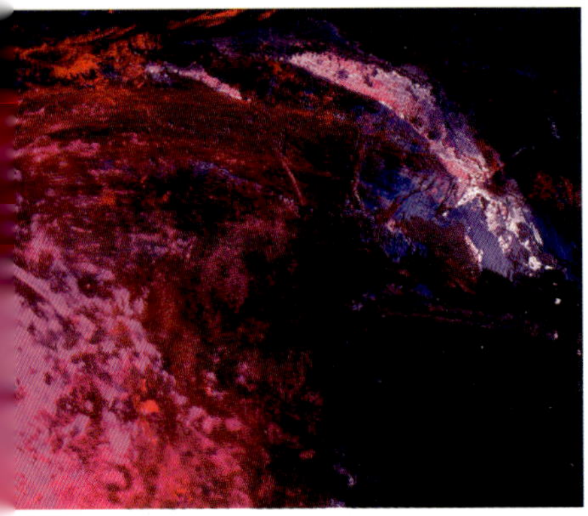

Was Paul looking for the man he had seen in his Macedonian vision when he set out to find the place of prayer on the riverside outside Philippi? Instead, he found a woman there—Lydia. When she heard Paul's teaching, she was deeply moved and eager to know more. She committed herself to God and was baptized, together with her whole household. Next she invited Paul and his companions to stay at her home. When they were reluctant, she insisted on it. As a result, their stay became a public, and recorded, endorsement of her faithfulness to the Lord Jesus.

Lydia is portrayed as a able and successful dealer in purple cloth. She could afford generous hospitality, and she had great social courage. Lydia was at the cutting edge of her culture. She is recorded as the first named Christian believer in Europe, and her home became the first 'home fellowship' on European soil. It seems reasonable to assume that Lydia became a leading member of the young fellowship of believers in Thyatira, though there is no evidence that she was a teacher or preacher. Paul's instructions later on to Timothy, who stayed with him at Lydia's home, were clear: 'I do not permit a woman to teach or assume authority over a man' (1 Timothy 2:12). I wish I could ask Paul what he meant and why he wrote that…

God Almighty, open our hearts to the good news of Christ, who gave himself to save us. And help us to commit ourselves to serve you in every way we are able.

Jezebel II

'Get up and eat! Cheer up. I'll get you the vineyard of Naboth the Jezreelite . . . He is no longer alive, but dead.'

1 Kings 21:7, 15

This is a horrific account of a powerful and wicked woman, a cheat and a liar who boasts in broad daylight about murder. She is a frightening caricature of pure evil. Even her husband King Ahab, who was notoriously greedy and godless, seems moderate by comparison.

Are there women like Jezebel around today? We hear more about men who rule with such utter contempt for justice. Is it because few women today have such authority? I think Jezebel proves that evil is without gender. Every person is capable of immense evil when they are absorbed only with themselves, when no one and nothing else matters. The spirit of Jezebel lives today in every oppressive and cruel ruler, in every political and social system that tramples the poor and disregards the righteous, where bribes determine what is right and wrong, where injustice reigns. O Jezebel, Jezebel, you are everywhere. But where is Elijah today, the prophetic voice we so urgently need to hear?

Whenever I lack compassion, lose my sense of righteousness, look down on someone else, stop caring about the poor and the oppressed, tolerate injustice and even promote it as acceptable, I become 'Jezebel'.

Lord God, we confess that each one of us can act like Jezebel and not even notice it. Forgive us! Instead, may our hearts burn with compassion for the poor and the oppressed. Use us as your instruments of justice. Make us sensitive to your will in everything we say, think and do.

Mary Magdalene I

[With Jesus were] also some women who had been cured of evil spirits and diseases: Mary (called Magdalene) from whom seven demons had come out...

Luke 8:2

This woman is the best known of Jesus' female followers. We are not told how she met Jesus, but he cast seven demons out of her. One demon is enough to destroy a person's life—but seven! Many illnesses were ascribed to demons in those days. I imagine that her condition would have presented as a form of severe mental illness. Perhaps she was violent or tried to destroy herself? We are not told the details, but it is clear that her life was shrouded in darkness, that she suffered desperately and, as a result of her condition, lived on the margins of society as an outcast—until she met Jesus, the incarnate Word, through whom everything had been created. He 'recreated' her, lifted her out of her darkness into his light, restored her humanity, filled her with hope and peace and freed her from pain.

Is it surprising that Jesus became the single focus of her life? By accepting her into his company, Jesus publicly restored her human dignity. Today she is honoured as Saint Mary of Magdala, a woman who was transformed by her contact with Jesus and was an eyewitness of the Resurrection. Like Mary who anointed Jesus with perfume and dried his feet with her hair, Mary Magdalene is still remembered today, wherever the gospel is preached. Blessed women!

O Jesus, we rejoice, with Mary Magdalene, that you are the wounded healer. We love you. Help us devote ourselves to you unashamedly with all that we have and are.

Dorcas (Tabitha)

'Tabitha, get up.' She opened her eyes, and seeing Peter she sat up.

Acts 9:40

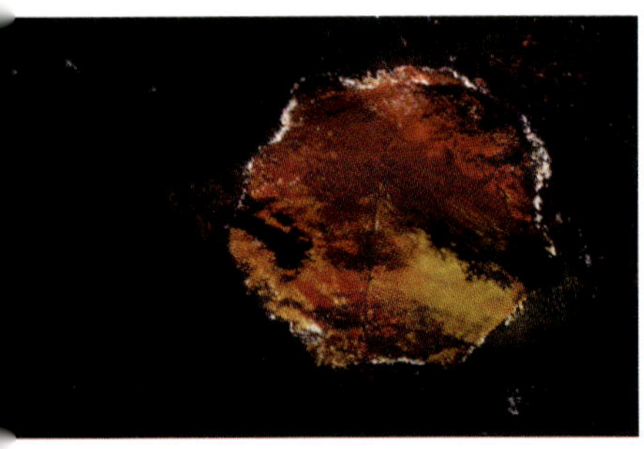

Dorcas is one of the few people the Bible mentions who came back to this life after tasting death. It is interesting that none of those 'resurrected' people have left us any account of their experience of death.

Dorcas is described as a disciple. In the community of Jesus and the early church, this was a rare honour for a woman. She was devoted to good work and acts of charity. Literally, she was 'full of good works'. When Peter arrived at her home, he found the widows weeping as they showed him the garments Dorcas had sewn for them. People's works tell their stories, even after they have died. I can imagine the scene, with the women deeply bereaved of their friend and helper, the one who listened to their problems. Dorcas's face is torn in two in this portrait. When Peter touched her, she was mended, restored to life, for the sake of the women she served. The left side of her face shows her surprised joy. Her restoration became a powerful testimony across the whole region. Today, Christian women called to the ministry of helps (diakonia), who use whatever talents they have been given, can transform the lives of the marginalized and suffering around the world. Do our churches encourage and honour such dedication?

Jesus, you are the Resurrection and the Life! Thank you for every woman who reflects your life-giving character by serving the needy and supporting those on the margins of society. Touch us, that we may be living witnesses for you.

Bathsheba

From the roof [David] saw a woman bathing. The woman was very beautiful . . . Then David sent messengers to get her.

2 Samuel 11:2–3

The portrait shows Bathsheba with a frivolous, playful expression, enjoying herself without a thought as to possible consequences. Surely David showed immorality beyond imagination in this story. First he had Bathsheba brought to him because he was aroused by her beauty, then he slept with her and afterwards, when it became apparent that she was pregnant, he plotted her husband's murder in order to marry her. Had she not become pregnant, would he simply have forgotten about her? I sometimes wonder.

Could Bathsheba have resisted the king's advances? We do not know, but we read that God judged David, and indirectly judged Bathsheba, through the death of the child they had conceived. Yet God also showed mercy to them—and perhaps particularly to Bathsheba—by choosing their second child, Solomon, conceived in love not in lust, to become David's successor to the throne. That would have safeguarded Bathsheba's position in the palace, even after David's death; it appears to express God's particular care for her. Although David apparently got away with murder, his life and household were marked by the affair. Corruption and lust for sex and power riddled relationships at David's court for the rest of his days, and beyond.

Lord, we confess that we too can easily fall into the traps of lust and momentarily be blinded to what is right or wrong. Give us discernment at such times. Purify our desires, strengthen our wills and help us not to deceive ourselves. And when we fail, Lord, thank you that with you we can find forgiveness.

The Samaritan Woman

'Come, see a man who told me everything I ever did. Could this be the Messiah?'

John 4:29

The text says that Jesus had to go through Samaria. Why? Devout Jews avoided travelling through Samaria for fear of being defiled.

While the disciples went to buy food, Jesus waited by himself at the town well. It is not difficult to guess why this woman-without-name came to the well on her own, perhaps also at an unusual hour, to fetch water. The portrait shows her as a woman with many 'faces'—after five husbands she was now living with a sixth man. Did Jesus interrupt his journey from Galilee to Jerusalem just to speak to her? His asking her for a drink was unusual behaviour for a man and especially for a Jewish man. In the conversation that followed, the woman was shocked to realize that he already knew everything about her. She tried to direct the conversation into 'safe' religious territory. But Jesus' words forced her to face the truth about herself and her deep spiritual need.

She understood that Jesus' request was not in the first place to get a drink from her, but to offer her the 'living water' of life. When she recognized God's Messiah, she was filled with such great joy that she rushed off to tell everyone in town the amazing news. Surely at least one of the reasons John recorded this story was because he saw her as a model of faith.

O Jesus, you hear our cry from afar, and you go out of your way to respond to our needs. Help us to understand your words so that we may be restored. Help us to generously share the blessings you give us.

Hannah

Eli thought she was drunk. . . . 'Do not take your servant for a wicked woman; I have been praying here out of my great anguish and grief.'

1 Samuel 1:13, 16

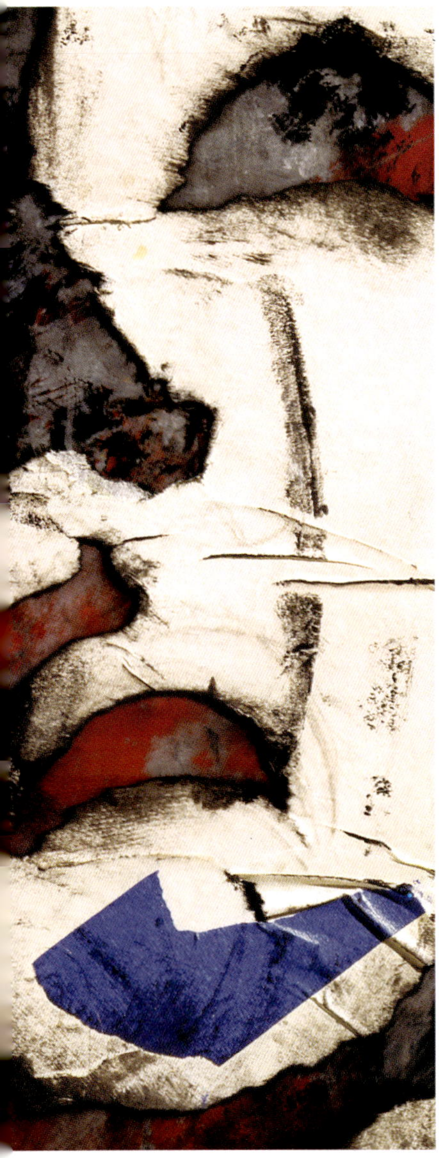

Sarah, in her barrenness, used her maidservant to conceive a child on her behalf. Rachel also attempted to conceive through her maidservant. But Hannah, though constantly insulted and provoked by Peninnah, only presented her desperate plight to God. As she prayed for a son, she vowed to give him back to God. Eli, who at first thought she was drunk because of her extreme anguish, unwittingly became a partner in prayer.

This portrait is the most abstract work in the book. The artist sought to express the intense cry of a devout person who is thrown completely onto God's mercy in her desperate need. As soon as her son, Samuel, was weaned, Hannah kept her vow. When she left him with Eli at the tabernacle, she once again prayed powerfully to God, in praise and worship. That prayer of Hannah was most likely in Mary's mind centuries later when she prayed her Magnificat.

I once told this story to a class of children. One child was very upset to hear that Hannah had left little Samuel at the tabernacle: 'How could she? Did she not like him?' Surely it was incredibly difficult for Hannah to leave behind her firstborn, but she honoured her vow. Hannah was a woman of faith, a poet and singer, a loving and caring mother, a remarkable woman and, surely, a praying mother.

Lord, you answer us when we cry out to you. You give us so much more than we could possibly expect. We praise your name! Amen.

Anneke Kaai Publications

English

- *Seeing a New Song: Painting the Psalms Connection* (Carlisle: Piquant Editions/ Nairobi: Word Alive Publishers, 2008)
- *From Beginning to End: Creation, The Ten Commandments, The Apostles' Creed, The Apocalypse* (Carlisle: Piquant Editions, 2007)
- *In a Word: Seeing What you Believe/The Image and Language of Faith* (Carlisle: Piquant Editions/Brewster: Paraclete Press, 2003)
- *The Psalms: An Artist's Impression* (Carlisle: Piquant/Downers Grove: IVP, 1999)
- *I Believe* (Carlisle: Paternoster Press, 1995)
- *Apocalypse* (Carlisle: Paternoster Press, 1992)

Dutch

- *Relaties met Psalmen: Schilderijen van Anneke Kaai* (Heukelum: Anneke Kaai/ Zoetermeer: Mozaïek, 2008)
- *Van Alpha to Omega: De Schepping, De Tien Geboden, Het Credo, Openbaring* (Heukelum: Anneke Kaai/Zoetermeer: Mozaïek, 2007)
- *Bijbelwoorden in beeld* (Zoetermeer: Mozaïek, 2003)
- *Psalmen in beeld* (Zoetermeer: Mozaïek, 1999)
- *Geloof in beeld* (Zoetermeer: Boekencentrum, 1995)
- *De Schepping in beeld* (Rhenen: Anneke Kaai, 1991)
- *Openbaring in beeld* (Rhenen: Anneke Kaai, 1990)

German

- *Ich bin und ich glaube* (Basel: Brunnen Verlag, 1995)

Spanish

- *Visión de una nueva Cancion* (Miami: Editorial Unilit, 2008)
- *De Principio a Fin: Creación, Diez Mandamientos, Credo de los Apóstoles, Apocalipsis* (Miami: Editorial Unilit, 2007)

CD-ROM

- *From Beginning to End—Van Alpha to Omega—De Principio a Fin: CD-ROM* (Carlisle: Piquant Editions/Heukelum, NL: Anneke Kaai, 2008)
- *Psalms and Bible Words—Psalmen en Bijbelwoorden: CD-ROM* (forthcoming in 2009)

Using Anneke Kaai's images

Artist's website: www.annekekaai.nl
Publisher's website: www.piquanteditions.com